DOMINIE READERS

The Red Magic Marker

Story by Janie Spaht Gill, Ph.D.
Illustrations by Bob Reese

DOMINIE PRESS

Pearson Learning Group

On Christmas Eve, Richard saw
a colored marker on the ground.

He picked it up and hurried home
to draw with what he had found.

First he drew a flower,
very large and red.

At once the flower
came alive!

"A magic marker!"
Richard said.

Richard drew a red bird,
but the red bird flew away.

Richard drew a red sports car,
but it did not stay.

Richard drew some red shoes,
which he slipped onto his feet.

Richard drew a bright red apple,
which he began to eat.

Richard drew a Santa Claus,
who popped right out and frowned.

"Tomorrow is a special day,
so I can't stay around."

"I must hurry to the North Pole,
for I have work to do.

Can you draw a sleigh,
and add a reindeer, too?"

Richard drew a sleigh with
runners long and red.

"For a brown reindeer,"
he thought, "I'll use a brown
marker, instead."

"If I hook the sleigh to the reindeer, the two should come alive."

Richard waited and he waited. "Nothing's happening," Richard cried!

"The reindeer can't come alive,"
Santa smiled and said.

"The reason is he's brown,
and both pictures must be red."

"Let me have the red marker,"
said Santa with a shout!

He drew a red nose on the reindeer,
and the pictures both popped out.

Santa gave a "Ho, Ho, Ho," then
flew into the sky.

Rudolph has a bright red nose,
and that's the reason why.

Curriculum Extension Activities

The Red Magic Marker

- Discuss how the story might have been different if Richard had found a marker of a different color. Have the children write or dictate the story and then draw illustrations.

- Brainstorm a list of different objects Richard could have drawn with the magic marker. Have each child pick something on the list and illustrate it. At the bottom of the page, the child writes a sentence. For example, "Richard drew a shoe, and it danced across the floor." Combine their pages to make a class book.

- Make a color wheel using primary colors of tempera paint. Dab paint of different colors along the outer edges of a paper plate and practice blending the colors. Discuss the new colors that are created when you spin the color wheel.

About the Author

Dr. Janie Spaht Gill brings twenty-five years of teaching experience to her books for young children. During her career thus far, she has taught at every grade level, from kindergarten through college. Gill has a Ph.D. in reading education, with a minor in creative writing. She is currently residing in Lafayette, Louisiana with her husband, Richard. Her fresh, humorous topics are inspired by the things her students say in the classroom. Gill was voted the 1999-2000 Louisiana Elementary Teacher of the Year for her outstanding work in primary education.

Softcover Edition ISBN 0-7685-2184-X
Library Bound Edition ISBN 0-7685-2492-X

Printed in Singapore
2 3 4 5 6 7 8 9 10   10 09 08 07 06 05

Dominie
Press

Pearson Learning Group

1-800-321-3106
www.pearsonlearning.com